Janet and John

The Parent's Guide

Published by
Star Kids Ltd
10 Greycoat Place
London SW1P 1SB

Prepared by *specialist* publishing services, Milton Keynes

First published 2001

Janet and John is a trade mark of Star Kids Limited

A CIP record for this book is available from the British Library.

ISBN 1 84258 0620

Printed in Spain

Contents

Part 1

Part 2

Part 3

Part 1

Welcome to Janet and John

Welcome to Janet and John

Janet and John is the most well known reading scheme in the UK. Over 71% of parents associate the phrase Janet and John with learning to read at home.

Star Kids are delighted to be able to publish a new and updated version of the children's classic for the new millennium. In developing the books we have focused on updating:

- the characters
- the storylines
- the settings
- and the key words.

Janet and John are children like yours with the good and bad features that all children have. They go to school, play with their friends and shop with their parents in the supermarket. Their lifestyle is one that children will find familiar.

It is hoped that as well as helping your children to read, Janet and John will also help thousands more to understand a little bit more about the world they live in.

How to use the Janet and John reading scheme

There are 8 books in the Janet and John Reading Scheme (two more than the original set of 6!). Each book covers a set of prescribed Key Words which deliver between 70 and 80% of the language your child needs to know in order to read with confidence.

Follow the books in order from 1 to 8. Encourage your child to get to know the books and the characters. Help them to notice that the books contain story pages, and also reference pages, indicated by a red border.

Read the book with your child, pointing to each word and sounding it out. Many of the words are phonic, meaning that a child can see the letter sounds and put them together to say the word. Some Key Words are not phonic, and can be more difficult to grasp. Repetition of these important words will help your child to recognise them and assimilate them into their reading vocabulary.

Gradually your child will become more confident with the words and the stories. Encourage your child to tell the story for themselves, seeing how many words they recognise. You can help with any words they don't know. Use the pictures to help you. As your child reads, it is helpful to point to the words as they are said, to reinforce the connection between the word on the page and the sound it creates. When your child is confident at reading the story to you, encourage them to point to the words on the page as they say them.

Remember that reading together is meant to be fun!

Read only for as long as you are both enjoying it, and provide plenty of praise and encouragement as your child learns to read.

The contents of each book

Each of the eight reading books contains three different Janet and John stories. These are separated by short reference, or non-fiction, sections, which are identifiable by their red border.

These reference sections are designed to help children recognise familiar words and objects. They are particularly important as children are expected to process a lot of written information in their education.

Help them to use the pages to look for specific bits of information in response to your questions. For example: Which bit of Tim's body does he hear with? Which of these objects are red?

From here your child can move onto other non-fiction forms of writing: information and 'fact' books, catalogue information or short articles written for children in magazines, comics and newspaper supplements. Understanding non-fiction helps children to understand the world around them.

Key Words

The Janet and John reading scheme is a Key Word scheme, which aims to use the words found most frequently in the English language in a repetitive and helpful way.

The Key Words used here are believed to make up approximately 70% of all language which your child will encounter. Over the first year and a bit of schooling your child will begin to become familiar with these words in their written form.

There are 100 Key Words in total in this scheme. These can be found on page 26. Each of the eight Janet and John reading books lists the particular Key Words used within it in its back pages – so that book 8 contains significantly more Key Words than book 1. Once you have read the story you can refer to the Key Words and see how many your child knows. If you are interested in how they have grasped a new word ask them to put it into a sentence. Phonic words are also included where appropriate, including some CVC words or Consonant/Vowel/Consonant words which are the easiest to sound out.

The Key Words in Janet and John will help you to unlock the world of reading for your child.

Part 2

You and your child
with Janet and John

Some basic tips on reading with your child

Find a time that is good for you and for them. Try not to start too late at night or when either you or they are rushed. A boiling pan downstairs or a baby crying does not help either of you to enjoy reading.

Don't feel pressured to read for long periods of time, or to read for a set time every night (although this can be helpful). Short bursts of fun time reading together can be more effective – and more enjoyable – for both of you.

Find somewhere with good light and that is quiet and turn off distractions like the TV or radio.

Talk about the cover of the book. Who is in the picture? What is the title? Who do you think Janet looks like? What do you think this book might be about?

Each Janet and John book contains three separate stories. If your child only has the stamina and enthusiasm for the first, stop there. If they are keen to carry on, you could read all three. Watch carefully for your child's reactions, and don't feel any pressure if it is not going as well as you might have hoped.

Look for other things to talk about:
• What do you think Janet and John will do next?
• Who is your favourite character?
• Can you make up a story about Janet and John?
• What do their voices sound like?

As a parent, it is important to understand that learning to read takes time and concentration. When you consider how many things a child needs to know to be able to read – the letters and sounds of the alphabet, the structure of words, and how books work – it's incredible how quickly children reach a level of confidence.

Like most skills, children learn best when they're having fun, so make reading a pleasure.

Help your child to understand, especially in their early stages of reading, that every letter, and some groups of letters, make their own sound when you read them out loud. If you sound out each part of a word, you can build up the whole word. It doesn't work for all words – it's better to learn how to spot some common words, especially the key words listed at the end of this book, without sounding them out. Reading the words around the one you're trying to read, thinking about the storyline, and looking at the pictures also help to predict a word.

Reading activities

- Get your child to organise their books alphabetically by author or title, or sort them into fiction and non-fiction.
- Challenge your child to find a word in a dictionary or a topic in a book while you time them. Can they improve on their time?
- Bake some cakes! You'll have to help with the weighing and hot oven, but your child should be able to read the instructions.
- Make a treasure trail with clues to read and a prize at the end.

Reading at school

During their day at primary school, children have a regular time devoted to reading, called 'The Literacy Hour'. Janet and John made their presence felt during similar times a generation ago. Now, during 'The Literacy Hour', time is divided into different types of work. Your child will spend some time with the whole class, perhaps reading together from a 'big book' which the whole class can see. Next, the whole class will be taught about how words or sentences are put together. Then your child will work in a group on a reading or writing activity, At the end of the lesson everyone will get together to talk about what they have learned.

Literacy in schools, reinforced by reading practice at home, works towards the point where your child is able to:

• read and write confidently

• see where they make mistakes, and correct themselves

• understand different sounds and spelling

• show a real interest in what words mean

• learn new words and use them

• know about different stories and poems, and be able to write their own

• describe to you different characters or storylines they have enjoyed

- understand different sorts of writing – not just stories, but facts, instructions and descriptions

- choose the books they want to read, and explain to you why they have made their choices

- use and develop their powers of imagination, inventiveness and awareness of the world around them through reading and writing.

At the end of Year 2, at the age of 6 or 7, your child will have an assessment at school. This assessment is through tasks – similar to normal classroom work – and informal tests carried out by the teacher. Many children are unaware that they are even taking a test! Reading is assessed by reading a book to the teacher or, at a slightly higher level, reading something and then answering questions about what has been read.

Your school will keep you fully informed on what your child is learning at school, but always feel free to ask for more information. Parent Teacher Associations help integrate parents into school life. It may be that you can arrange to sit in on a part of your child's day – it would be a good thing to find out about!

Other reading you can do

Websites

The internet contains a wealth of resources for parents, with information on what you can expect at school and how you can help at home. You can find further information, and organisations which exist to support the parent.

Here are some suggestions.

• Advistory Centre for Education: www.ace-ed.org.uk/

• BBC: www.bbc.co.uk/education/home/index

• Book Trust, The: www.booktrust.org.uk

• Child Literacy Centre, The: www.childliteracy.com

• Educate the Children: www.educate.org.uk

• Federation of Children's Book Groups: www.fcbg.mcmail.com

• Government Education Department: www.dfee.gov.uk

• Janet and John websites: www.starkids.uk.com and www.janetandjohn.com.

• Literacy Trust: www.literacytrust.org.uk

• National Grid for Learning, The: www.ngfl.gov.uk

• Parenting Education and Support Forum: www.parenting-forum.org.uk

• Parent's Information Network: www.pin.org.uk

• Parents Online: www.parents.org.uk:

• Year of Reading: www.yearofreading.org.uk

How to find further resources:

• ask your child's teacher for suggestions

• look for tips and ideas in one of the many parenting magazines in newsagents or bookstores

• your local library will have details of parent and child events in your area, as well as facilities to encourage your child to read at home

Part 3

Janet and John:
past and present

Janet and John: a very British reading scheme

If it is not already a pub quiz question, then the original publication date of Janet and John soon will be. Believe it or not, the grainy covers and watercolour artwork first brought us Janet and John in 1949. Adapted from earlier American models, Janet and John were given a truly British makeover and presented to parents and teachers as the companions for children learning to read.

Janet and John seemed to capture a child-like idyll of post-war Britain. As the country got back on its feet, the characters came to symbolise the innocent hope of a new generation. At the time, the illustrations and stories were a true breath of fresh air. Many of us remember characters and scenes from the original editions. Though never truly representative of the communities in Britain, Janet and John did fit with contemporary images of children at play. We remember them as carefree, bright, with more than a touch of the fairy tale about them.

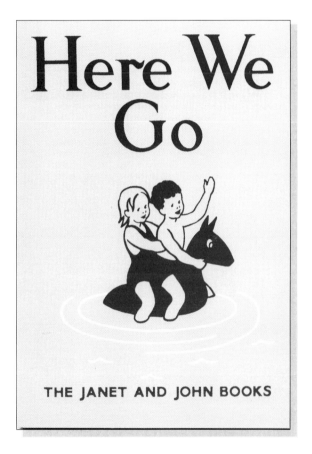

If you have one or two original editions tucked away in the attic, why not dust them off and indulge yourself in a nostalgia trip? What memories do the pair bring back? How different is the world for our children and grand children today, compared with Janet and John's?

Janet and John: the golden years

In the 1950s and 1960s, Janet and John became the best-known and most-loved reading scheme in the land. Teachers and parents could choose from two versions of the six books: a whole-word scheme and the alternative phonics approach. In the end, whichever you chose, what counted was the formal structure and close attention paid to the key words every child needed to learn.

Compared to the enormous and complex schemes used today, Janet and John can seem simplistic. And yet it worked. Millions of children learned to read using those six little books.

WORD LIST

JANET AND JOHN BOOK ONE contains 49 ' look and say ' words, and each of these words appears (on the average) 9 times. The phonic work contributes another 17 words to the reading matter. Sixty-six different words are therefore used in building up the total reading content of 516 words. (Twenty-seven of these 66 words have already been introduced and familiarised in the introductory book *Here We Go*.) The phonic tables, which deal with the five short vowels and give practice in every consonant occurring in three-letter words, list a further 126 words (not used in the stories). The total number of different words presented in *Book One* is thus 192.

The vocabulary used in the stories, in the order of its introduction, is:—

2. This, Janet, *is*	19. *us*
3. John	20. aeroplanes
4. See, Mother, and, the, *can*	21. said, fly, *up*
5. Father	22. *it*
6. little, *dog*	23. down
7. come, to	24. good, slide, *on*
8. look, fast, *at*, *run*	25. went, he, *top*
9. jump, my	26.
10. I, skip, like	27.
11. after, you	28. very, of
12. kittens, one, two, three	29.
13. play	30. horses, ride
14. basket, *in*	31. here, too, *ran*
15.	32. may
16. boats, a, *big*, *has*, red	33.
17. want, go	34.
18. me, *let*	35. thank, *had*
	36. for, good-bye

NOTE.—The words in italics are examples of the phonic work tabulated on pages 38, 39, 40. The other words are at this stage ' look and say.'

J. & J. 1. *Back.*

In a recent survey, 71% of parents with young children recalled learning to read with Janet and John. It is an astonishing figure, possibly too high. But it bears witness to the impact Janet and John had in this country. Abroad too, especially in countries like Australia, New Zealand and South Africa, Janet and John found a home and an admiring audience.

Inevitably, Janet and John not only dominated the market place, but also set the tone and standard for others to follow. Imitators did come, often with some success. But none matched the heights reached by the lovable characters.

By the end of the 1960s Janet and John's artwork was beginning to look out of place in the Beatles era. Life was faster and noisier: closer to the psychedelic than the watercolour. Janet and John seemed to be living on borrowed time.

Janet and John: out of favour

The big debate about how children learn to read began in the 1960s and exploded in the 1970s. Janet and John fell foul of the fashionable trend towards using real books instead of phonic schemes. More to the point, the stories, settings and language were

Janet and John face expulsion

Daily Express April 21 1976

dated and did little to promote our multi-cultural society, or positive role models for women. In

Outlaw Janet and John!

Daily Mail April 21 1976

an era of political correctness, Janet and John were singled out for criticism and sometimes contempt.

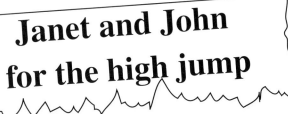

Janet and John for the high jump

The Guardian Nov 30 1976

As teachers experimented with the new way of doing things, and parents followed suit, Janet and John struggled to maintain a presence in this country. Now labelled 'old-fashioned', only traditionalists kept faith with the six books. By the end of the 1970s, they seemed to be on the brink of disappearance forever.

Curiously, however, nobody remembers the books they learned to read with in the 1970s.

Whatever their correctness, they lacked the emotional appeal that had so characterised Janet and John. Similar to many children's television characters today, the new books seemed to lack staying power and went as quickly as they came.

Janet and John: the 1980s and 1990s

The past two decades have seen Janet and John find a new home in society. Whilst only a few hundred copies of the original editions are sold each year, the phrase 'Janet and John' has passed effortlessly into our contemporary language. It is used as a metaphor for something very simple and straightforward; even sometimes in an ironic way in the sense of an idiot's guide!

Politicians looking for a catchy phrase guaranteed to capture the voters' imagination have been quick to use Janet and John to complement an agenda about returning to traditional values.

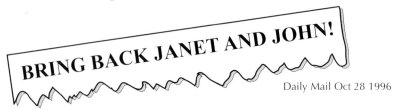

BRING BACK JANET AND JOHN!

Daily Mail Oct 28 1996

If the pendulum swing is not going all the way back to the 1950s, it has certainly seemed headed in that direction. Politicians, teachers and parents feel that some of the traditional values do have a place in today's world, which is more complex and threatening than they can ever remember before. With so much uncertainty perhaps it is inevitable that we would look to bring back images from our past, giving us something we can hold on to and understand.

Almost every week, some newspaper or magazine carries a reference to Janet and John. It is a term often used on radio programmes. Even if we no longer use the six original Janet and John books to teach our children to read, we use their memory to colour our conversation.

Janet and John: reborn

Bringing Janet and John back to life has been our passion as publishers for some time. During 2000, Star Kids acquired the rights to the characters from the daughters of the original author. They were also the original publishers, James Nisbet and Co.

We have re-drawn the characters, re-written the stories and re-thought the reading scheme. But, despite these changes, we hope we have kept to the original spirit of the books: simple, free from ideology and jargon, and with a direct appeal to children's own experiences.

We have added a good deal of humour, as much for parents as for children, in the belief that learning to read should be exciting and fun, not a drudge. The original six books were of varying lengths. We have chosen to publish eight books of even lengths so children will find a more regular progression in their learning.

In these books our hope is that parents will find an easy-to-use-tool for supporting their children's emergence as readers. With all the attention paid to schools and schooling, it is too easy to forget that a child's best teacher is often their parent.

Key Word Reading

Below are listed the Key Words contained in this book.

Key Words are those that make up most of the English language.

It is important that your child knows these words. They are often repeated for emphasis, and used with other phonic words - that is, words which can be sounded out by children.

a	in	had	are
of	to	at	have
and	is	out	they
that	was	her	for
he	the	his	see
went	I	we	go
my			
		their	not
		get	off
		do	today
		on	big
		put	back

30

31

Will the new-look Janet and John still be around in fifty years? Probably not. But we hope that what the characters stand for will remain, with some future publisher re-creating them again to fit with a mid-21st century world. But just to show Janet and John can mix it with the best technology the world has to offer today, you can find them at http://www.janetandjohn.com!

Key Words used in Janet and John

Below are listed the key words that make up most of
the English language. Each Janet and John book
identifies in the final pages which of these are used in
their stories. It is important that your child knows these
words and recognises them when reading.

a	I
in	my
of	then
to	with
and	come
is	had
that	me
was	some
he	are
it	has
the	one
went	there

at	their
have	not
out	get
they	be
her	once
saw	last
this	call
for	will
his	could
see	all
we	three
go	off
little	here
she	our
when	live
about	can

make	what
do	so
as	after
today	them
on	now
big	got
very	because
put	other
made	like
take	came
next	you
from	did
back	an
two	time
into	old
by	us

over	July
look	August
new	September
down	October
away	November
too	December
him	one
but	two
were	three
said	four
January	five
February	six
March	seven
April	eight
May	nine
June	ten

Other Janet and John books you can buy

As well as the eight Janet and John Reading books, there is a range of Janet and John titles for children aged 4–7 to enjoy at home. Fun, colourful workbooks – each containing stickers and a 16-page reading book – are available in the three key areas of learning: maths, reading and writing. Look out for these titles in a bookshop near you.

Age 4

Maths	*Reading*	*Writing*
Play All Day	Colours	On the Farm
Where is Tim?	Dress Up	Visit Ben's School

Age 5

Maths	*Reading*	*Writing*
All The Year Round	Go Swimming	New Bikes
Size and Shape	Go to the Park	Play Shops

Age 6

Maths	*Reading*	*Writing*
Go Camping	The Art Show	Ben Gets Lost
Sports Day	The Visitors	Dad Goes to School

Age 7

Maths	*Reading*	*Writing*
Decorating	New Skates	Looking After Mum
The Cake Stall	The Old School	The Boat Trip